On My Knees

#positionofcomfort

On My Knees
#positionofcomfort

Janice Genath Washington Steve

XULON PRESS ELITE

Xulon Press Elite
2301 Lucien Way #415
Maitland, FL 32751
407.339.4217
www.xulonpress.com

© 2021 by Janice Genath Washington Steve

All rights reserved solely by the author. The author guarantees all contents are original and do not infringe upon the legal rights of any other person or work. No part of this book may be reproduced in any form without the permission of the author. The views expressed in this book are not necessarily those of the publisher.

Due to the changing nature of the Internet, if there are any web addresses, links, or URLs included in this manuscript, these may have been altered and may no longer be accessible. The views and opinions shared in this book belong solely to the author and do not necessarily reflect those of the publisher. The publisher therefore disclaims responsibility for the views or opinions expressed within the work.

Unless otherwise indicated, Scripture quotations taken from the King James Version (KJV) – *public domain*.

Paperback ISBN-13: 978-1-6628-2145-5
Ebook ISBN-13: 978-1-6628-2146-2

Table of Contents

"On My Knees" #positionofcomfort 1
The Visit from an Old Neighborhood Acquaintance .. 3
The Last Birthday Visit 5
Mother's Wit 7
Taken by Man (Peace) 9
Life, the Great Teacher........................... 11
The Bone-Chilling Call 13
Given by God (Peace).............................. 17
A Family of Dreamers.............................. 19
What Happened to the First Forty-Eight Hours?..... 21
#Position of Comfort 23
On My Knees 25
The Thing that Led to the Thing 29
My Dealt Hand 31
Decisions... 33
The Verdict 35
The Morning After 37

"On My Knees"
#positionofcomfort

Ver'mon D. Steve was a homebody growing up; he made the comment as a little boy that he would never leave home. Then life happened—he learned some hard lessons, went to a local technical college, and graduated at the top of his class with a certification in welding. He moved around for a while, then moved to the city in South Carolina where he was born, reared, and attended school; the place he loved with his whole heart.

Working two jobs to support his lifestyle, he seemed happy.

The Visit from an Old Neighborhood Acquaintance

Ver'mon and I (I, being Janice Genath Washington Steve the person Ver'mon called "Mother"—out of our four children, he was the only one that called me Mother) would communicate daily via talk or text, most days with just a "How are you, Mother?" and ending with, "I love you." We talked one day after he had been in his new place for three months. Most of the conversation was about a young man, who we knew of from the neighborhood he grew up in, stopping by and they became reacquainted. Ver'mon told me this young man had spent some time in prison, had been recently released, and had nowhere to go. The young man asked if he could stay for a few weeks until he could get on his feet. Ver'mon, being a fun-loving, believing-there-is-good-in-everybody, happy-go-lucky kind of guy WITH THE GIFT OF HELP, allowed him to stay.

The Last Birthday Visit

Ver'mon and his best friend visited me on his birthday. This was the norm: he would bring a bunch of live flowers, thanking me for allowing him to be born. However, on October 3rd, 2015, he brought this beautiful, colorful pot of artificial chrysanthemums.

Jokingly, we (the family) referred to them as "funeral flowers," not knowing what the future held, or the history of chrysanthmums. As I was writing, I got curious about their history and learned that in the United States, they represent **respect** and **honor.** In Asia, they signify **life** and **rebirth,** and, believe it or not, in some countries they represent **death** and are the flower for funerals (NYBG 2020). His last words to me that evening were, "Mother, if you don't see me anymore, I want you to know I got my life right with the Lord." Those words had me filled with mixed emotions, both happy and sad. I did not want him to see me cry; after all, it was his birthday.

I was shedding happy tears because he was professing Jesus as his personal savior, but I was sad because of the first part of his sentence ("If you do not see me anymore"). His friend went on to say, "Mrs. Steve, he is making me nervous; all he talked about coming up here is that I need to be saved because we could die at any time."

I do not know what had my baby thinking about death—could it have been being robbed that day and his peace of mind being taken away? Did he have an unspoken encounter with the roommate, or, like me with my dreams, was God preparing him? They had to drive forty-five minutes back home in the rain, and, of course, "*car accident*" came to my mind because in October 2015 South Carolina was experiencing lots of rain. It was reported in that week we had over fourteen inches. After hugs and kisses, my last words were, "Text me when you two get home." They did, and it eased my mind.

Mother's Wit

I visited Ver'mon's home one week before our lives would change forever. That day we laughed and talked about him saying he would never leave home; about his hardwood floors being shinier than mine; about how much he loved his new job at a local metal sign-making company, using his welding certification and doing some of what he was passionate about—**creating things**—and the fact that he was robbed about a month earlier. He felt he was set up by a woman he thought was a friend while he visited her home.

He told me she went to go buy cigarettes and left the apartment door, which automatically locks when pulled shut, ajar; three masked men came in and, at gunpoint, took his ring, watch, and his payroll for that Friday from one of his jobs, which was in his pocket. He also talked about who he thought the three men were. Then he said, "I do not care about the money and things they took. I can get that stuff back. What upsets me, Mother, is that they **took away my peace of mind.**"

I also got a chance to meet the man he had given a place to live. He was not at home when I got there, but he came in later during my visit. Ver'mon introduced me as his mother, to which the young man gave me a big hug and said, "Mrs. Steve, I remember you!" We both said, "nice seeing you again," and he took a plastic grocery bag he came in with to the back room, where he had an air mattress and a television that sat on the box in which it came. Yes, I had already had a peek. He called Ver'mon to the room, stayed in for just a few minutes, and left. I did not get good vibes from him and shared my feelings with Ver'mon, who then said to me, "This is not going to work. I must get this dude out of this house. He is up to no good."

He never said what the "no good" was, and I did not ask. I said, "Ver'mon, he is not paying you rent, so just tell him you are sorry, but it's not working." I found out later Ver'mon's attempt to get this man out of his house is what caused him to show what I will always believe were his true colors.

Taken by Man (Peace)

The saying, "Hindsight is 20/20," allows me to see what my baby son (although thirty-six years old) meant that day when he said, **"The only thing that upsets me, Mother, is that they took away my peace of mind."** These words break my heart today, as they did then, to know that the most peaceable individual I know had his peace of mind stolen.

My baby, the man who was anointed by God with the gift of **help**. Since he was a child he possessed a servant's heart; there was nothing anyone in need could not get from him, if he had it to give. It may have been all he had, but his words were, "They need it more than I do." His last dollar, he has given it; shoes off his feet, he has given them; his coat off his back, he has given it. As a teen, there were a few times he sacrificed himself by breaking curfew to help someone that was stranded. He just wanted everyone to be "happy".

He was robbed thirty days before he was killed, and the people he thought were responsible were some of the same people whose names were called and eventually convicted of accessory after the fact of murder. They assisted in moving his body after he was shot, once in the face and four to five times after he fell backwards out of his door to the ground; they also poured gasoline on him and set him on fire in an attempt to get rid of evidence. There are things I went through in life that I never told my parents, and I hoped my children would never have to experience anything like it that would take away their peace of mind.

Life, the Great Teacher

In my profession as a registered nurse, I spend a large majority of my time doing what I was taught in college, along with twenty years of on-the-job training it took to save lives. If it turned out to be a failed attempt, I was always left with the question, "Was there anything more I could have done?" And to think, a twenty-one-year-old man who, from my understanding, had never been in trouble before, would allow himself to be talked into waiting in the dark, in the home of a strange man, for twenty-eight minutes (the police report stated) to take a life is beyond my comprehension. I believe he was chosen because he did not know Ver'mon. If he did, he would not have been able to kill one of the most loving people anyone could ever meet; just the thought takes my breath away. It breaks my heart over and over to think that my baby had to live his last days on this earth with the thought that any day he could be killed by a madman.

The Bone-Chilling Call

On October 26th, 2015, at about eight o'clock at night, I got the call from my son's best friend that would put me on my knees. The caller said, "Mrs. Steve, Monie is missing, and I think something bad has happened." My insides grew cold and remained that way for a while. It was a chill that made me hug myself but could not be comforted; a chill that made my teeth chatter, even though I was not cold. It was the worst kind of chill. Again, in my profession, fever and chill is a sign that something is going wrong in the body. The chill that night made me know something was wrong.

It was a chill that lasted for months, as we first looked for "the **missing man Ver'mon Steve,**" as the media referred to him. Then, in January 2016, came the confirmation that bones that had been found in a desolate, marshy area called **Pee Patch,** a place I had never heard of in my life and will never forget for the rest of my life, were those of the missing man, my baby son, thirty-six year old Ver'mon D. Steve. The chill remained with me through Thanksgiving 2015 in sunny Florida, at the home of my sister and brother-in-law where the family had come together to get away from the heart-stopping reality at home. The chill was there through Christmas and into the New Year as we waited to put his remains to rest.

Given by God (Peace)

I cannot tell you when the chill went away but it did, and I think then is when I realized what the peace of God truly feels like. As I write, it is ironic that the very thing that was stolen from my son by a madman in his last days—peace of mind—would be the thing needed from God to make it through my last days, however long that may be.

> **And the peace of God which passeth all understanding shall keep your hearts and minds through Christ Jesus. (Philippians 4:7)**

Day after day, the peace of God is what helped me to make it through the almost four months, which felt like a lifetime, we had to wait to lay my baby's remains to rest.

How do you have peace when someone you love dearly has been taken away from you, forever, by a madman that was given a place to live when he had nowhere to go?

Some may say he was not named the killer; no, not by the evidence, but in my mind and heart, **he will always be the man that was responsible for my son's death— ALWAYS!** But that's the next book, *The Real Killer.*

A Family of Dreamers

As I think back, the call was not a surprise; however, the information was bone-chilling. About a week before, I had a dream that my husband died. In my dream, he fell to the floor lying on his back, blood gurgling from his mouth, as he took his last breath. For lack of a better description, he rolled out of his body, (over which I was kneeling), smiled, and repeatedly said, "Baby I'm ok, I'm ok." There was the shadow of a man in a dark corner of the room that I could not make out. Then I woke up.

In the same week, if my memory serves me correctly, my mother shared with me one morning a dream she had. "Jan," she said, as I am, affectionately known by my family, "I had a dream about you last night that was not good." She went on to say, "I answered the phone and a lady asked to speak with you. I don't know what she said, but you started crying, and crying, and I woke up." I guess it goes without saying we are a family of dreamers; that is why I say the call from my son's friend was not a surprise.

The call from Ver'mon's friend initiated action. Our oldest daughter, Angel, drove me forty-five minutes from our home in South Carolina to the police station near where Ver'mon lived to file a missing person's report, which was an experience all by itself. I realize everybody has policies to uphold, but I was made to feel they did not want to be bothered. I was determined Ver'mon D. Steve was not going to be just another young, black man out of the way. In my mind, that was the thought of the law enforcement; at the time there had been about eight murders of young, black men that were yet unsolved.

What Happened to the First Forty-Eight Hours?

It took a few days to get the ball rolling. The police had to be convinced that Ver'mon was not out gallivanting somewhere. My son could not be found, and the police were not listening to me. He was not the child who would leave town for any reason without letting me or his sisters know where he would be. He never wanted to be the reason his mother would worry.

#Position of Comfort

I was in the city where my son lived by day, and on my knees at a loveseat in our living room by night. It was my "**position of comfort**." In bed, it felt as if I would stop breathing; sitting in a chair was uncomfortable. I did what I had to do to maintain my family, but at that chair, on my knees, was where I could be found. **I never remember being able to pray**, but I was on my knees.

Being a nurse, like being a child of God, is a part of me. I am always able to share examples because these are two of the areas I have learned great life lessons.

As a nurse, I cannot help but think of the patients I have had the honor of caring for. I was trained to change the position of a patient who was unable to turn him/herself every two hours or less as needed. I recall, on one occasion, caring for someone who had been diagnosed with right side lung cancer. Whenever the patient was placed on their left side, they would become very agitated until they were turned back to the right side. This was very frustrating for me because one of my focuses was on preventing skin breakdown, and the patient needing to be on the right side most of the time to be comfortable was hindering my ability to be a great nurse, or so I thought.

Allow me to digress. I would like to take this opportunity to do a little of what I will call Nursing 101. Ninety-nine percent of my critical thinking skills were developed on the medical surgical floor. After being educated by one of the great physicians on staff, I learned that because the right side was the affected side, the left side needed to be up, giving the unaffected lung more room to expand; hence allowing the patient to take in much needed oxygen and therefore becoming less agitated—**the position of comfort.** That moment was one of my greatest learning experiences and allowed me to become a better critical-thinking nurse and patient advocate.

On My Knees

I have been a religious person since I was a child. I was taught the right Christian way early in life, starting in Pilgrim Ford Missionary Baptist Church where my father was a member, and I joined at the age of twelve. I had a choir director, Mrs. Queen Esther Young (who has gone on to be with the Lord). She would only accept our best. There was also a deacon, Amos Riley, who would from time to time see me and ask, "You alright?" For me, that meant was I doing the right thing. I had a profound respect for him and the position he held, as I still do. Later in life, I accepted Jesus as my personal savior and learned for myself the power of prayer; on my knees was the only place I knew to be.

On my knees was where I could think; on my knees was the only place that kept me from running with no destination; on my knees was where I was able to keep myself together when I got calls saying things like, "Your son's body is this place or that place." There were many calls, but after the police department investigated each, they were found to be false information. On my knees was where I had to be during the times I tried to contact one of our other children and they could not be reached. My heart would start racing until I was able to hear from them. The situation had caused me to become more of an overprotective, paranoid mother. On my knees was where I needed to be to maintain the face needed to lead my mother, Rebecca, who lives in the home with us, to believe I was ok, so she could be ok. On my knees was where I had to be to keep me.

For whatever reason, it seemed as long as I appeared ok, the rest of the family was ok. If at any time I had a "bad day," it was bad for everyone in the house. Our granddaughter Da'nae'ja ("The greatest granddaughter in the world," my hus-

band calls her, praising his own pond) who loved her uncle so much would retreat to her room. My mother would begin inconsolable crying. Our baby daughter April, who had withdrawn from college, was home, and she and her sister would become more upset; my husband Joe turned into Rambo, and our oldest son De'me'tre'o—who was already the boot-leg private investigator out on patrol—went about seeking who he may destroy of the four whose names had been called in the disappearance of his brother. This was because they were on the run and had not been located by the police at the time.

I did not realize it then, but I know now that I was not on my knees for myself only, but for my entire family. Like the person mentioned earlier with lung cancer, positioning was very vital for me. On my knees at that chair was where I felt I could breathe, where I felt I was being held by the only person who could hold me: God. **That was my position of comfort;** on my knees was where I could shut out the world and just be. As I said before, I do not ever remember praying while there, but I had to be there. I now understand the words in an old song sung by the Five Blind Boys of Mississippi that states,

"I am sending up my timber every day," because on days like the days I was having at that time, I needed my timber to be in place. I am so grateful and thankful that **God loves me so much;** sometimes just being in His presence is all I need, and He takes care of the rest.

While we were out looking for what I called, as the quote states, "a needle in a haystack," there came another reason for me to be on my knees. In November, I got a call that my father was found unresponsive on the floor while an inpatient in one of the local hospitals. This put him on life support for eight days, in another hospital over an hour away. Now, from the city where my son was killed, where I was looking and listening, to my father on life support with a questionable recovery.

The Thing that Led to the Thing

Before my life got turned upside down, I was working on an invention. I had it in the hands of the production manager; lots of money paid, patent pending. I presented one thing to the invention helpers and they offered me something else. I turned it down because what they wanted to produce for me was not the idea I was holding on to for almost thirty years. This was my baby, my millionaire maker, and when I was financially able, I put my invention into the hands of this invention help company.

In the midst of losing my son, I looked up one day and on a popular talk show was my invention, owned by someone else. My other baby was taken away. I was devastated, disappointed, and my trust was shattered. I wanted to give up on life at this point. I did not know how or what to feel. The person telling the talk show host about the invention was about twelve years old, had not been around long enough to experience or have knowledge of what they were saying they had invented. I felt I had been ripped off. On my knees was where I had to be. This is not a claim, but is this invention helper taking my money and my idea? With a self-investigation, I found the new owners had made millions. I took the risk of reaching out for help with my invention, and I lost, or so it may seem.

While on my knees, I heard Bishop T.D. Jakes tell the story that he told one of his sons, referring to a "what-if" situation where one thing did not work out for him. Bishop said he told him, if one thing did not work, then it would be the thing that leads to the thing.

This book is my **"thing,"** and here is my affirmation. I am thankful and grateful for my first bestseller.

Then a call from my job came, asking if I wanted them to hold my position. I had taken a leave of absence while we were dealing with my son's disappearance and alleged murder. It was the place where I could say, without reservations, I served wholeheartedly for about twenty years. "Hello Janice, we are hiring, and I want to know if you want me to hold your position." At this point in my life, there are no surprises; anything can happen. I took a deep breath and responded in faith; "It is obvious to me that this job has meant more to me than I meant to it. No, don't hold my position." I thank God, because to this day I have not had to regret my answer. On my knees was where I needed to be to make it through this test. On my knees, my position of comfort.

My Dealt Hand

My baby son was an up-and-coming rapper. One song he left words to states, **"I got my mind on my money, grill all gold, God dealt me a hand I could never fold."** I must say I thank God for my dealt hand. It has not been an easy hand to play, but **I thank God for His perfect peace**; the peace that kept me on my knees, and in my right mind through it all. I would like to say to people, especially women who wish to walk in other women's shoes: **"You don't have a clue what it takes to be me. Make sure you are willing to pay the same price."**

Three years after Ver'mon's murder, we had our week in court, which I think was strategically planned. Allow me to digress for another educational moment for some. If you ever go through anything that has a possible lawsuit attached, file a complaint while you wait for the facts, being cognizant of the statute of limitation in that state. I feel the city where my son was killed failed him that night. I say this because there were turns of events that were mentioned by people in the community and 9-1-1 reports that never came to court. More on this in my next book.

I put more miles on my vehicle from October 2015 to January 2016, driving back and forth, than the years living in Mississippi and coming home to visit, and I was home often. When I was not at the hospital with my father, I was in the city where my son was killed. With everything in me, my son's murder was not going to become an **"unsolved murder,"** not if I could help it. I am thankful for the prayers of many, from near and far. People that I did not know would seek me out and say, "I have you and your family in my prayers." I was, and still am, grateful and thankful, for every prayer. The police had names and they needed to do whatever it took to find them. That was my sentiment.

I would like to say to the world I have learned that you can be hurt so badly that no matter what, it does not matter; this does not have to be death. I could elaborate from experience, but I will allow you to use your imagination. When you have experienced the ultimate anything, nothing else matters much. Yes, things bother you and cause you to call on the Lord, but the sting has been taken away. I became numb after my son's murder and had to ask God to help me. I had a "Why should I care?" attitude. I never became angry with anyone, not even the man that pulled the trigger, or the **"real killer"**; but at that point, I felt I had given all my love away and did not want a refill.

Decisions

To the people who choose to take the life of someone who is not attempting to take yours, **you are making a permanent decision based on a temporary situation**. I do not want to sound prejudiced or partial, but to young, black men, please, for your life and the life of the person you point a loaded gun at, **think twice before you pull the trigger, because the other life you save will be your own.** You could never imagine what you do to a family as a whole, and to the individuals who had their own special, or not-so-special, relationships with the person you take away. You choose to make a permanent decision; permanent because the person taken away will never return, and caught or not, your life will never be the same.

The Verdict

This takes me to the last day of the trial: two broken mothers leaving the courtroom shedding bitter tears, me with mixed emotions from utter disbelief to overwhelming sorrow, as both families were escorted out. Officers surrounding us as we walked in separate groups, but in the same direction to our vehicles. The young man who pulled the trigger of the gun that took my son was sentenced to life plus twenty-five years. Only a mother who lost her child could imagine what she was feeling at that time. In my expression of empathy for her, I was told, "But you will never get to see your son anymore; at least she will get to visit hers." On some of the faces with her, I could see the expressions of anger, and the same on some of the faces with me.

His mother and I, at the time I would speculate, were being looked upon as the leaders of each pack, and the vibes sent from the two of us could have sent this crowd in another direction; another teaching moment. Young people, there are individuals in your circle who are looking for you to be the first to just say no to drugs, violence, teenage sex, drinking, smoking, bullying, cyberbullying, going against the wishes of your parents/ the adults in your life, and all the other things that today's world has to offer. They are forcing you to become an adult before your time. It may only be you and one other, and I am sure the thought is scary. With God, however, two can put ten thousand to flight. **Young people, there is an old person inside of you depending on you. Depending on you to be the best you, you can be.**

I say only a mother who had lost a child could imagine what she was feeling; I felt she was crying the tears that day, that I cried at my son's funeral three years before. All I wanted to do was hug her, and I did. I asked one of the officers that was escorting her family if I could approach her, and she agreed. At that moment, I felt she was feeling the same thing I was feeling. Each of us was sorry the other had to go through what they were going through. In the parking lot that day, I feel the hug we shared in some unspoken way mended our hearts toward each other. It allowed us to say without saying, meaning different things to both of us as it meant the same thing to both of us: **"I am sorry your son was taken away."**

The Morning After

I often wonder what the four involved in my son's murder think each moment of each day. There is not a day that I do not think about my son. Some days I laugh and many I cry. It is now five years later, and some days it still does not seem real. There is not a time at a family get-together his name does not come up. I have had a few people to say to me, I am sure innocently, "At least you had two sons." And each time my thoughts are, *but I only had one Ver'mon*. Ver'mon D. Steve can never be replaced; in my life and neither in the lives of all the people he impacted. This young man, after he went through his finding-himself phase, you could find him making people laugh or leading someone to the Lord. Because he was not perfect, there were a few whose last nerves he got on, but in the end, he was about keeping the peace.

He lived the Scripture, "If it be possible, as much as lieth within you, live peaceable with all men" (Rom. 12:18). His favorite words, when he would part company, were, "I love you and there is nothing you can do about it." These are the words scripted on his headstone: "At a young age, he parted our company, loving each of us, and there is nothing we can do about it."

Over the past five years, positioning remains extremely important to me. I am not still at the loveseat on my knees, but I continue to search for my position of comfort. A few days after hearing the words, "Ver'mon is missing and I think something bad has happened," God brought who I will refer to as an adopted deacon safely to our home, and took him back safely to his, over thirty miles away. I was told he was only to drive in his neighborhood, an eighty-some-year old, well respected, God-fearing **gentle-man**, who has since gone on to be with the Lord, to give us these words: "**We**," meaning Christians, **"are not exempt."** That is, from the troubles of this world; but if we allow Him, God will position and keep us. Not every situation will be comfortable, but if we trust God, He allows us to find, our **position of comfort**.

CPSIA information can be obtained
at www.ICGtesting.com
Printed in the USA
LVHW071144310721
694127LV00010BA/319